NO RISK, NO REWARD

Adventures of a Golf Course Architect

David V. Ferris, Jr., ASGCA, RLA

First Edition

ISBN: 978-1-66786-285-9
1. Biography. 2. Golf. 3. Architecture.

Written by David V. Ferris, Jr.
Interior design by David V. Ferris, Jr.
Cover design by Pam Germer

Thank you to my mother and brother
for all of those evening rounds
that brought us together and inspired one to dream.

David Ferris, on-site with John Sanford and Jack Nicklaus at the Naples Beach Hotel and Golf Club, 2016

Table of Contents

Foreword by Yukio Takahashi   vii

Introductionix   ix

Chapter 1:
From the Big Leagues to the Back Nine   1
    Yin and Yang   3
    Imhotep's Footsteps   6
    Home Field Advantage   9
    Around-the-Horn   10
    Reclamation   12
    ASGCA   13

Chapter 2: Yin and Yang   15
    Kona Country Club   15
    Great Sand Dunes   16
    Waimea Country Club   18
    Garden Valley Golf Club   20
    Regent Miyazaki Country Club   22

Chapter 3: Imhotep's Footsteps   24
    Maritim Jolie Golf Resort   24
    Little Venice Golf Resort   25
    Taba Heights Golf Resort   26
    Palm Hills Golf Resort   28
    Madinat Makadi Resort   30
    Hacienda Bay Golf Resort   32

Chapter 4: Home Field Advantage   34
    Banyan Golf Club   34
    Hobe Sound Golf Club   35
    Hunters Run Country Club   36
    Juliette Falls Golf Club   38

    Naples Beach Hotel & Golf   40
    Banyan Cay Resort & Golf   42
    Spring Run Golf Club   44
    Mission Valley Country Club   46
    Pointe West Country Club   47
    Wilderness Country Club   48
    Eastpointe Country Club   50
    Miami Shores Country Club   52
    Wycliffe Golf & Country Club   53
    Pembroke Lakes Golf Club   54
    Atlantis Golf Club   56
    Breakers West Country Club   57
    Vero Beach Country Club   58
    Madison Green Country Club   60

Chapter 5: Around-the-Horn   62
    Apple Mountain   62
    The Quest   64
    The Sawmill   66
    The Brookside Club   67
    Caguas Real   68
    Duxbury Yacht Club   70

Chapter 6: Reclamation   72
    Granite Links   72
    Trump Golf Links at Ferry Point   79

Epilogue   90

About the Author   92

Foreword

John Sanford and I met when I was planning to build a golf course on an old buffalo ranch I purchased called Zapata Ranch in Alamosa, Colorado. I asked him to come and see the site and we inspected the 110,000 acres of land. Although we did not speak each other's language, I sensed that he shared the same excitement I had, thinking about designs for developing a new golf course in this beautiful landscape. As we stopped at the fence for a moment, I remember John kneeling to pick a wild asparagus and eating it raw. He then picked another, gave it to me, and gestured for me to eat it. Strangely, I felt a strong bond between us, and we've been working together ever since.

"Kanpai!" Mr. Takahashi, his long-time associate Fumiyo Okuda, and John Sanford

John invited me to play on many different courses. I had already owned several golf courses in Japan, but came to realize that golf courses in the U.S. were very different. John is an exceptionally humble man and I am forever grateful to him for professionally showing me the true game of golf and personally welcoming me as his friend. It has been a fun and educational journey working with him and has certainly been a joy for me to watch him succeed in becoming one of the best golf course designers in the world. I sincerely wish all the best for John and am looking forward to seeing more of his designed golf courses.

Yukio Takahashi

Introduction

Think of your favorite golf course, and then think of the criteria you used to determine it. Consciously or subconsciously, we use three basic components to evaluate any golf hole: conditioning, aesthetics and strategy.

Conditioning, the quality of turf and a golf course's overall upkeep, starts with its infrastructure, e.g., irrigation, soils and drainage. It is critical for a superintendent to control water going on and off the golf course. A golf course architect's design must successfully deliver these components to ensure the future viability of the golf course. The other aspects of conditioning, such as maintenance, equipment, fertilizers, etc., rely upon the continuing financial investment of the owner. Once a golf course opens, the need for future improvements and the golf course architect doesn't disappear. Golf courses are a living part of our environment, and like any living thing, they deteriorate over time.

Aesthetics of a golf hole relates to the natural and built environment it's designed around and into. An outstanding golf hole is an artistic composition created by the golf course architect's use of colors and contrasts derived from a palette of green grasses, white sand bunkers, blue waters, native ground covers, and an array of opulent flora set amongst sculpted shapes. A golf course architect will try to use a site's unique natural features to create aesthetics (and strategy) whenever possible, but when a site offers few opportunities, the designer must rely on their own creativity. Take for example Pebble Beach's iconic 18th hole; its aesthetic beauty is created by masterfully incorporating the Pacific shoreline, a unique feature in-

capable of replication anywhere else. On the flip side, the 17th hole at TPC Sawgrass is also an iconic hole, with its island green front side pot bunker and bulkheading, but because its aesthetics are manmade, the hole can be, and has been, recreated.

Strategy is what defines a great golf course, but what is strategy? The job of the golf course architect is to create obstacles that challenge and require players to judge how far and where to hit a shot, while factoring in natural elements such as wind. John and I are firm believers in risk/reward strategy. The term "risk/reward" originates from the financial world as a measure of how much one is willing to invest in exchange for potential return. We have adopted it as our golf course design philosophy. When a player steps onto the tee, we want them to contemplate how much of a hazard they're willing to take on, be it a bunker, lake or other obstacle. If a player successfully executes a more aggressive shot, their risk is rewarded with a shorter distance on their next shot and a better angle into the green. Hazards should not be placed within the golf course to penalize, but rather reward the player who successfully executes a shot that challenges the hazard. A golf course should give the golfer space to play; there should be a way around each hazard and not a "forced carry."

The golf course architect's first step in every project is to understand the goals and objectives by working diligently with stakeholders. Time is also spent on-site reviewing topography, vegetation, drainage, existing features and general conditions. These critical components form a design's

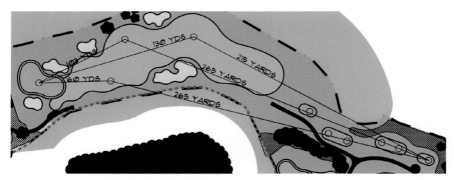

Tee shot angles and length—an important part of our philosophy

While green side hazards dictate strategy, we angle greens and create hole locations that enhance the risk/reward shot quality. With today's turf varieties and improved maintenance practices, our slopes for areas with hole locations are between 1 and 3 percent (1.25–3.5 inches of vertical change over 10 horizontal feet). Green size will depend on various factors such as hole length, volume of play and environmental conditions, but typically our greens range from 4,000 to 7,000 square feet.

foundation and shape the project's future. After all of the analysis and input has been synthesized, the following golf course features are developed: **TEES** are an important factor in making golf courses playable. Designing multiple sets of tees allows the hole to be played from varying lengths, so the golfer can select the appropriate tee based on their abilities. With today's ball and club technology, there seems to be no end to the potential length of a golf course from the back tees, but our forward tees typically play from 4,000 to 4,500 yards, which we believe is most appropriate for today's higher handicap players. Tee angles are also given careful thought, with back tees typically requiring a more challenging shot over or around a hazard than the middle and forward tees.

Tee sizes are critical when trying to maintain quality turf, especially in places like South Florida, where courses typically get the most play in the winter, when turfgrass growth is slowest. For this reason, we try to maximize their size: typically 7,000 to 8,000 square feet per hole.

GREENS must provide a consistent playing surface and are the most maintenance-intensive aspect of the golf course. We typically design our greens to be approximately 80 percent pinnable.

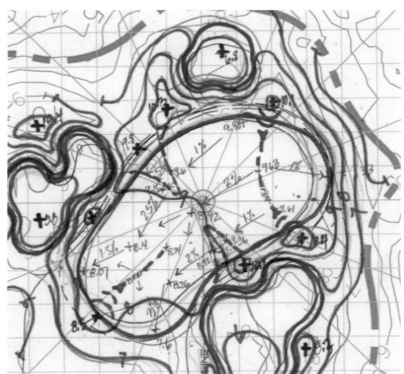

Green detail sketch with proposed features and contours

BUNKERS are not only an important strategic component of the golf course, but they also create striking visual contrast of white sand set against the deep green turf to form the golf course architect's artistic palate. They inform the golfer where to hit (or not hit) their shot, creating a "road map" for the player to follow. While John and I do not adhere to a "one size fits all" bunker style, we do design all of our bunkers to be a strategic visible hazard. A project's site, goals and objectives, and budget constraints will determine the number, sizes and style of bunkers.

WATER HAZARDS were not an inherent part of golf's origin on the great links of Scotland, but they have become a vital component in golf course development worldwide. Whether it's removing excess water or adding an irrigation system, water is the most critical ingredient for maintaining healthy turf. In South Florida, lakes are designed not only to store water for a course's irrigation system, but also to collect runoff from the golf course, and often from surrounding developments, then convey excess storm water to a series of water management control structures and canals.

Depending on the project goals and objectives, lakes can be enhanced with rock features, waterfalls, bulkheads, flowering aquatic plantings or a combination of these. When a golf hole is set against native elements, such as a lake, hillside or a stand of colorful vegetation, it should expose the natural beauty of the site and accentuate the hole's strategy without striking fear into the

Master plan for the restoration of Donald Ross's North Fork Country Club in Cutchogue, New York

golfer. Forced carries over water can frustrate golfers, slow down play and should be avoided; there should always be a way for the golfer to get around the hazard. As Alister Mackenzie once wrote, "The best golf courses can be played with just a putter."

LANDSCAPING provides a visual backdrop and can enhance a hole's strategy, but placement is critical. John and I were trained as landscape architects. We understand the beauty and importance of integrating trees, palms, shrubs and ground covers within the golf course. We develop planting plans and locate landscape material on-site to insure healthy turfgrass is maintainable and course playability is not negatively impacted.

CONSTRUCTION OVERSIGHT is a responsibility John and I pride ourselves on. All great golf courses are a result of the designer spending time on-site to oversee the construction. From clearing to grassing, we are intimately involved in every facet of the course's construction.

The early stages of construction are often the most creative part of the process, when the character of the golf course begins to take shape. Since every hole is unique, with its own issues to solve, each visit is a collaborative effort with the contractor, allied consultants, owners, club and staff.

Apple Mountain's par-3 5th hole with its apple-inspired green complex

Rough shaping is the transformation of dirt into the basic forms and shapes of the new golf course features. Before infrastructure is installed, rough shaping must be approved by the golf course architect. The detailed finish work is the refinement of the rough shaped features and is reviewed and approved prior to grassing. During this very important approval process, slopes are checked for conformance with documents and verified with digital levels, proper location of landscape plantings is verified, bunker sand lines, putting surfaces and cart path tie-ins are examined, and surfaces are checked to ensure they are free of rocks and debris.

Rough shaping at the Naples Beach Hotel

John, like me, literally "grew up" in the golf business, forming his unique perspective that a golf course should be economically, environmentally and socially sustainable. As an avid player, John understands the importance of incorporating risk/reward opportunities into his designs and that the best architects are students of their predecessors. He's worked with some of the most respected architects and renovated revered layouts, all with a deep respect for the history of the game and the courses it is played on.

Having worked with John since 1997, I have seen how these fundamentals are incorporated into all of his designs. John has navigated his career like he navigates a golf course, taking on risks to gain a greater reward. This book is a celebration of his work that allows us to look back on his artistic compositions and accomplishments, while leaving room for new chapters and a conclusion that is hopefully a long way down the road.

John working with shaper Marty Dye at Juliette Falls

From the Big Leagues to the Back Nine

John Sanford grew up around baseball. His father, Jack Sanford, was the National League Rookie of the Year in 1957, pitched a shutout against the mighty Yankees in Game 2 of the '62 World Series, and finished runner-up to Don Drysdale for the Cy Young after his 24 wins that season, which included 16 straight wins—a feat only six other pitchers have ever accomplished. So how does someone who spent their childhood growing up around guys like Willie Mays and Willie McCovey end up turning a passion for golf into an accomplished golf course design career?

After Jack retired from baseball, he took on a new career running the golf operations at President Country Club, a new 36-hole golf complex in West Palm Beach. This is where John fell in love with the game, practicing and playing most days when he wasn't helping his dad at the club. The family's neighbor Bill Mitchell was a golf course archi-

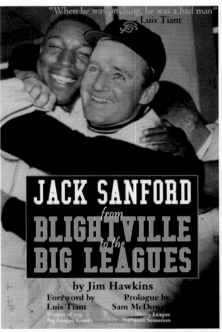

The story of John's dad was published in the 2016 book *Jack Sanford: From Blightville to the Big Leagues,* featuring Willie McCovey and Jack on the cover

tect who designed notable courses in the Northeast and in South Florida. During his own career, John renovated several of Bill's courses, with a unique respect for the design and the man.

The foundation of a good golf course architect is a good player. This is true for John, an accomplished amateur who grew up playing with guys like Mark Calcavecchia, Steve Hart and Ken Green, went on to play golf at Louisiana State University, has won local and state tournaments, and been a single digit handicap since Nixon was in the White House. If playing golf is considered the foundation to his career, then his education represents the pillars. While attending LSU, he studied landscape architecture, a program that offers courses in design, art, plant materials, construction, grading and drainage, all pertinent to golf course architecture.

John giving Dad a few pointers while he was a pitcher for the San Francisco Giants in the early 1960's

After graduating, John returned home to work for a land planning–landscape architecture firm and became a Registered Landscape Architect in the state of Florida.

John's golf course design career can be broken down like a classic Fitzgerald novel, with a beginning, middle and end (yet to be written). The introduction, or beginning, starts with a young man who had recently taken ownership of a West Palm Beach planning firm, Planning/Design, Inc., when a client came through the door with a resort project located on a Caribbean island.

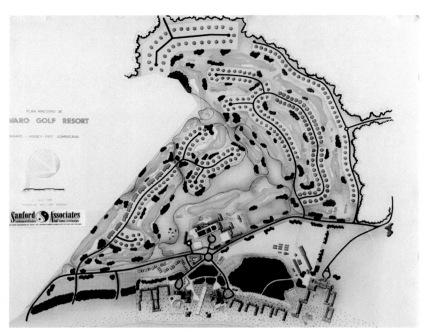

Bavaro Beach Resort, ccompleted in the 1980's and still operating today

By the mid-1980s, John had designed residential communities, shopping centers and gas stations throughout South Florida when he was asked to join a meeting regarding a resort project in the Dominican Republic that changed everything. John had collaborated on several projects with a talented local architect, Ricardo Gonzalez, who was working with a college friend developing a master plan for hotels, a casino, restaurants and pools along a mile-long beachfront on the east end of the Dominican Republic. The plan had maximized development along the beach but left an unused large track further inland. Never one to miss an opportunity to promote the game he loves, John suggested building a golf course to allow the owner to maximize the use of the property.

As John recalled,

"This was my golden opportunity. I immediately suggested we design the inland area with a golf course and could plan more hotel rooms, casinos, restaurants, etc. around the course to take advantage of the views. At that moment I had no idea I would end up designing the golf course, but when the owner asked who could design the golf course, I raised my hand and the rest is history."

An early planning project of John's, the Wellesley Inn on Palm Beach Lakes Blvd. in West Palm Beach, Florida, with the original office for Planning/Design, Inc. shown in the background

Yin and Yang

Yin and yang is an ancient Far East concept of dualism describing how seemingly opposite forces are actually complementary and interconnected in the natural world. This is true with John's career, as there was a time when he was balancing land planning and golf course design projects. Sanford Golf Design, then and today, pays tribute to that professional dualism by adopting the yin and yang symbol in its logo.

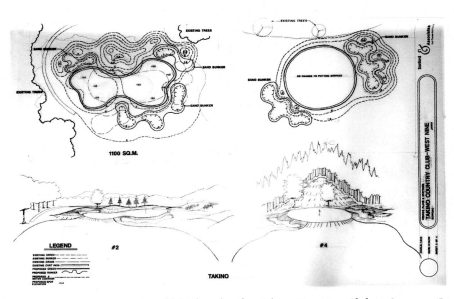

An old Mylar plan for Takino Country Club in Sapporo, Japan

The partnership that forged John's career blossomed out of a series of serendipitous events. John's stepbrother Mark was attending University of Hawaii and working at Waialae Country Club when he met a Japanese businessman named Yukio Takahashi, known by friends as Mr. T, through Mr. Norman Inaba, a Hawaiian who assisted with Mr. Takahashi's U.S. golf course developments. When Mark discovered they were looking for a young architect to work with, he arranged a meeting back in Florida.

"I was 28 at the time," John recounted, *"and had a BIG night before we were to meet and play golf. I was not feeling very well. It was a rocky start to say the least, and it was all I could do to keep playing. The game started to come around and I ended up under par that day. I have no idea how that happened, but it certainly got Mr. Takahashi's attention. We spent the next week playing golf, going out to dinner and getting to know each other. We are still best of friends today."*

Despite speaking different languages, Mr. Takahashi was impressed; the two hit it off and John became Mr. Takahashi's architect. To forge this new business partnership, John visited Japan and, as John recalls, found himself reluctantly showing the people of Japan his "inner Elvis."

"Mr. Takahashi sent me a first-class ticket to Tokyo. We had not discussed business during our first week together, so I thought, 'This is my chance.' After I arrived at Narita Airport, we went straight to a karaoke club in Ginza to meet up with a dozen Japanese businessmen. The only singing I had ever done was in the shower, so as I walked in the door and was handed a microphone, the anxiety level rose. I explained I couldn't sing and definitely didn't know any Japanese songs. The club owner spoke English and informed me they had 'Yesterday' by the Beatles and it was my turn to sing. After completely butch-

John and Mr. Takahashi playing at the Taba Heights Golf Resort on the Gulf of Aqaba in Egypt near the Israeli border in 2009

ering the tune, I received a standing ovation from the entire bar. I would return to Japan many times and always enjoyed the Japanese people and culture."

Over the past 30-plus years, the two have worked together on dozens of projects, including Great Sand Dunes in Alamosa, Colorado, which may be the most unique project they collaborated on. By spending a significant amount of time on-site, they determined the best locations for greens and other golf course features, skillfully fitting the course into the natural landscape. The golf course utilized a gravity feed irrigation system and was shaped with minimal disturbance, eliminating the large earth-moving operations typical to golf courses designed in that era. This approach also allowed for preservation of native trees and vegetation. Sadly, the course was taken over by the Nature Conservancy

and left fallow and decimated.

"I have fantastic memories of building the course in Alamosa. It was a gorgeous piece of property, all sand based and perfect topography for golf. We literally went out and found 18 holes on the ground and removed only three trees in the process. I

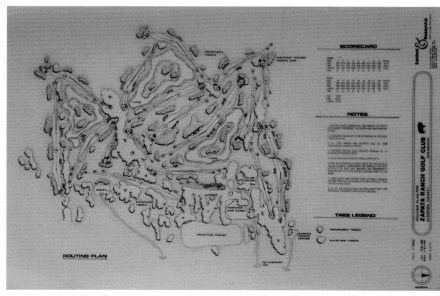

A 1988 plan for Great Sand Dunes, originally called Zapata Ranch Golf Club

Great Sand Dunes in Alamosa, Colorado, a unique layout John did for Mr. Takahashi, with a minimalist approach that was ahead of its time

had no idea how lucky I was to be building a course on that incredible site. I remember picking raw asparagus from the ground under the cottonwood trees and eating them as we walked the site. Mr. Takahashi got a real kick out of that."

Mr. Takahashi, Lee Trevino and John in the late 1980s while collaborating on the design of the Regent Miyazaki Golf Club

Many of the projects John worked on with Mr. Takahashi never made it off the drawing tables, but those that did proved to be quite spectacular. Regent Miyazaki Country Club was co-designed with legendary golfer Lee Trevino. Holes carved out of mountains and greens benched into steep slopes provide a stunning backdrop for this shot-maker's course. While working with Mr. Trevino, John learned one of Lee's design approaches: the finishing holes should not be the hardest holes on the golf course, because he'd have to give a shot to an opponent. Additionally, most matches never make it to the 18th hole, so the 15th or 16th holes are the most likely place for deciding a match. John has incorporated this approach into his designs ever since.

Probably the most visually striking of Mr. Takahashi's projects is Kona Country Club, located on Hawaii's Big Island. Carved out of the lava shoreline, golf holes are set adjacent to the Pacific Ocean's crashing waves. It is also home to remains of the historic Keauhou Holua Slide and site of the Makahiki games, ancient Hawaii's equivalent of the Olympics.

The back nine on the club's Mountain Course is an original John Sanford design; similar to Regent Miyazaki, its holes carved out of a mountainside. The Ocean Course was designed by William Bell in the mid-1960s. Fifty years later, John and Mr. Takahashi restored the championship course and improved its drainage and irrigation infrastructure.

Kona Country Club, Kona, Hawaii—Ocean Course Hole 3

Imhotep's Footsteps

Imhotep is considered ancient Egypt's first architect, and his name has come to mean "the one who comes in peace." In the mid-1990s, John walked in his footsteps when he got involved with a resort project on the southern tip of the Sinai Peninsula. Through an old friend of his father's, John was introduced to Hussein Salem, an Egyptian tycoon, former general in the Egyptian Army and close friend of President Mubarak. He had made a fortune as an arms dealer, real estate developer and all-around entrepreneur.

Mr. Salem owned a resort hotel on the tip of the Sinai Peninsula that was doing well, and the area was starting to become popular with Europeans. He also owned the local utilities and was told he could no longer pump sewage into the Red Sea due to the negative impacts on the area's world-renowned scuba diving industry and coral reefs. Mr. Salem decided he would build the best resort in the Sinai, including a golf course

that would double as a spray field. With water a precious commodity, Sharm's desert course was designed with less than 80 acres of irrigated turf, a far departure from the typical 150 acres that traditional courses irrigate.

Back when the client was trying to determine the best site for the development, John recalls an idea he had to get a better view.

"I was invited to visit Mr. Salem and assist him in locating the best site along the beaches of Sharm el Sheikh. I flew to Cairo, climbed aboard his G4, and in 20 minutes we were landing in 'Sharm.' We jumped into his Hummer and started driving through the desert looking at sites. I was surprised how much topography there was along the coast. It was difficult to determine which site was best for Mr. Salem's project, and after a few days of driving around, I spot-

ted a parasailer just off the beach. I asked if I could parasail close to the beach as high as possible so I could get a good aerial view of the properties under consideration. Next thing I knew I was 300 feet above the boat, and at times over land. It was exhilarating and a great way to see the contours in the land, which made it easier to pick the best site. Mr. Salem built a massive resort on that property and my first course in Egypt."

John's bird's-eye view while parasailing to find the best site for the Sharm El Sheikh resort golf course

As golf was new to Egypt, so was its construction. To build the course, a U.S. contractor was hired, and large shaping and earthmoving equipment was loaded on a ship for transport to Egypt. During one of John's early visits to the construction site, he had the opportunity to learn the life-and-death importance of payments from a contractor to the Bedouins.

John was on the property reviewing rough shap-

Sharm El Sheikh, originally called Naama Golf Resort, an original John Sanford design from 1997, located on the southern tip of the Sinai Peninsula

ing when a large Mercedes came ripping across the desert. The car pulled up and a young Bedouin dressed in full Hijab jumped out. He found John and started yelling in Arabic.

As John recalls,

"I was younger then and was not going to put up with it, so I told him to back off or he would have a problem. One of the Egyptian foremen immediately jumped in-between us and spoke to him in Arabic. After a few minutes he calmed down, pointed his finger at me, got back into his car and drove away."

The translator later informed John that the young man was one of the local Sheik's sons, collecting their appropriated percentage of all construction activities in their territory. This practice is common and well known in the Sinai, but the American contractor building the course had not paid the "baksheesh."

"Since I was directing the work, he assumed I was the contractor and came to me first," John said. *"Later that night I asked what he was yelling and found out he was 'going to kill me if I didn't pay before sunset.' I can assure you the Sheik was paid immediately!"*

John's Sharm El Sheikh project helped bring golf to Egypt, became the vacation home for Egyptian President Mubarak and has hosted many foreign leaders. John recalls one of his visits during the Clinton administration:

"The resort was one site of Middle East peace talks, and I met President Mubarak several times. One time, President Mubarak, Mr. Salem and I had tea on the 18th green with Egyptian military surrounding us on rooftops. Mr. Salem became a good friend; he told great stories and we had lots of fun together."

In the mid-2000s, John was visiting a new site new mega development near the Red Sea.

As John recalled,

"It's a beautiful area with deep blue water on one side and mountains on the other. We had recently completed Madinat Makadi Golf Resort not far down the road and it

was already rated the best course in Egypt. This new project was planned for multiple courses, so the owners had my attention."

Taking in the cultural sites of Egypt with a visit to the Great Pyramid of Giza

One of the golf sites was directly on the beach, with a three– or four-meter escarpment. As he walked the site with the engineers, planners and owners, the conversation revolved around that shore being accessible by the Israeli army with amphibious vehicles due to its low escarpment.

John said,

"As we continued to walk, the conversation transitioned from English to Arabic. When I asked what they were talking about, there was hesitation. One of the engineers reluctantly informed me that the Egyptians had

planted landmines here to stop the Israelis from coming ashore. I politely asked if the mines had been swept, and the engineer replied, 'No... not yet.' I went into full panic mode. I don't know why but I started running as fast as I could to the site vehicles. Obviously it wouldn't have mattered, but I wasn't going out while walking. When the group finally caught up to me, they were still laughing hysterically."

New friendships, one of the many benefits of working in Egypt

While working in Egypt, John formed a partnership with Cairo businessman Saiid El Derini, helping John become the leading golf course architect in Egypt. Over the next 25 years, John designed and built several more projects, including Madinat Makadi—ranked the number one course in Egypt; Little Venice—a 9-hole course located on the Red Sea; Taba Heights Resort—*Golf Inc.*'s International Development of the Year; Hacienda Bay Resort—located on the Mediterranean Sea near the WWII site where General Rommel was defeated; and Palm Hills Resort—a collaboration with Nicklaus Design, adjacent to the Pyramids of Giza. To this day John considers Saiid and many others he's worked with in Egypt some of his best friends.

Home Field Advantage

Working close to home is an advantage not every golf course architect gets to enjoy. Many spend weeks at a time traveling state by state, country by country, to design and build their projects. John has done his fair share of traveling, but since completing Ferry Point, he's been focused on working close to home. The benefits are twofold: the first is more time to spend with family, friends and playing golf; and the second is the added attention that John's projects receive, as he is on-site and managing things on a daily basis.

John's golf course design work in South Florida started in the early 90s with his renovation of Breakers West. Despite getting his foot in the door, the decade was defined by his work in Michigan, Texas and internationally. There were occasional planning exercises, like the Polo Club, but it wasn't until two new projects, Madison Green in Royal Palm Beach and Pointe West in Vero Beach, that John was truly able to enjoy working closer to home.

Over the next two decades, John left his mark on golf in Florida. Whether it was a complete blow-up with new routings, like the ones for the West Course at Wycliffe Country Club, Banyan Cay Resort & Golf (with Jack Nicklaus) and the Naples Beach Hotel (with Jack Nicklaus), or a smaller renovation at Miami Shores, they all got John's foremost attention, artistic touch and unparalleled services.

One type of renovation that truly captivates John's interest is restorations. With the utmost respect for his predecessors and a curiosity to learn from and be inspired by the layouts that popularized the sport, he always strives to help clubs preserve their past while implementing improvements, with a keen eye on future users. John has been fortunate to work with Jack Nicklaus, Lee Trevino, Bruce Fleischer and Ken Green, but it's probably the restoration of the great tracks created by the likes of Dick Wilson, Bill Mitchell, Joe Lee, George Fazio, Herbert Strong, Wayne Stiles and Donald Ross that, though less noticed by golf course design enthusiasts, are some of the projects most appreciated by the clubs he's worked with.

Around-the-Horn

"Around-the-horn" is a baseball term to describe the ball making its way around to every base in the infield. Similarly, John has designed courses around-the-world. While some projects, such as a golf resort in the Canary Islands, never made it past the drawing table, others found seemingly insurmountable hurdles. Those that were completed are a testament to the strategic, playable, and fun golfing experiences John creates.

was a co-design with long-time friend and PGA Tour player Ken Green. Apple Mountain is a community that offers golf in the summer and skiing in the winter. The championship course plays on and off the ski hill, which provides stunning visuals and a challenging yet fun golf course for players of all skill levels.

"My father always said it's better to be lucky than good. In the early 1990s I was asked to fill in at a PGA seminar in Palm Beach Gardens. I gave a brief talk about master planning golf course communities. On the way out I was approached by three guys from Saginaw, Michigan. They were planning a golf community and were avid

Breakers West in West Palm Beach, John's first Florida renovation

John's work in the 1990s included three new golf courses in Central Michigan: The Sawmill, The Quest, and Apple Mountain. The Sawmill was John's second project in Michigan, with a routing that winds its way around natural wetland and the area's pine groves. The Quest

golfers; one was a PGA Pro. I invited them to play the next day, and to this day I don't know how I birdied the first four holes and was six under on the front. Needless to say, it was a great day. Phil, Dick and Andy became good friends and had a blast building The Sawmill Golf Club. During the construction I met a local contractor, Mike Bierlein, who had just purchased an old apple farm, and subsequently we built Apple Mountain just a few miles away in Freeland."

The only golf course John designed in Puerto Rico is a resort course in Caguas, a small city located in the Central Mountain Range. The front nine holes is routed through the flat areas adjacent to the Turabo River, and the back nine holes traverses the steeper slopes to the south. In addition to having a flamboyant developer who ended up serving time behind bars in the middle of construction, the project also involved a near-death experience for the project manager.

"I made regular site visits, stayed in San Juan and commuted to the site each day," John recalled. *"One day I stayed late and walked the construction site until dusk. As I was leaving the site, I noticed the project manger's SUV parked on the side of the road. Naturally, I stopped to see what was happening and found the driver's door open, lots of blood in the road, and no driver. I called his phone but no answer, then called another manager and found out Jaime (PM) had been shot in the head while leaving the site. Long story short, Jaime survived and a month later was back on the job. Although he could identify him, the shooter was never caught."*

A mid-90s planning graphic for the Polo Club in Boca Raton, Florida

Reclamation

John has taken on two very technically driven projects that required the reclamation of landfills, importing millions of cubic yards of fill material, working with historic preservation efforts, preserving wetland, venting methane gases, mitigating settling that can occur on landfills as garbage breaks down, extensive permitting, and in-depth project timelines that spanned more than five years. While landfills do not present the ideal natural setting that golf course architects aspire to find, they do provide a canvas for creating a revenue-generating recreational facility out of an otherwise-unused large parcel of land. Since the Granite Links and Trump Golf Links at

Granite Links Golf Club with the Boston skyline in the distance

Ferry Point stories are as remarkable as the courses themselves, they are shared in their own chapter (see Chapter 6).

Trump Golf Links at Ferry Point with the New York City skyline in the distance

The American Society of Golf Course Architects

Through the first half of the 20th century, golf in the United States experienced tremendous growth, and with it came the need for more courses. This in turn created growth in the profession of golf course architecture, and led to the formation of the American Society of Golf Course Architects in 1947 by Donald Ross, Robert Bruce Harris, and other influential golf course architects of the day. The organization's core mission is to foster professionalism, support design excellence, help grow the game, and expand the opportunities for its members to better serve their clients and the game of golf.

John with the great Jackie Burke, Jr., at the ASGCA Annual Meeting

In 1998 John joined the ASGCA as its 187th member. As an active member, he served on various committees, including the Strategic Planning Committee and its board of governors. In 2014 he was elevated to the executive committee, and over the next couple of years he served as secretary, treasurer, and vice president before taking the reigns as the organization's president. Under his leadership, the ASGCA expanded and strengthened its brand, increased interaction with allied organizations, and built on its partnerships with national media outlets. John has made several appearances on the Golf Channel representing the ASGCA and continues to work with the USGA on their distance study.

According to Chad Ritterbusch, ASGCA executive director since 2004, John served ASGCA and the profession with great distinction.

"John actively participated in the creation of ASGCA's first official Strategic Plan back in 2006. This document helped ASGCA advance in a host of ways," he said. *"It's also when many ASGCA leaders—I among them—really began to see how special John was. He was smart but didn't flaunt it. He wanted the best for the organization but wasn't self-righteous. He led but in a collaborative way."*

"As I look back at the last 15 years and the great progress that ASGCA has made, I

see John's fingerprints everywhere," Ritterbusch continues. *"We are more effective, welcoming, and even fun because of John's participation and influence. I'm proud to have served him as president. And I'm just as proud to call him a friend."*

John's career has taken him many places and exposed him to people and cultures he may not have otherwise seen. The images and stories found in the following chapters are an affirmation to the vision and skills he brings to each of his projects.

Presenting the ASGCA's Donald Ross Award to President George H.W. Bush

Making golf great again at the ASGCA's 2017 President's Dinner

2

Yin and Yang

Kona Country Club
Kona, Hawaii

Carved out of the lava shoreline, with golf holes set adjacent to the Pacific Ocean's crashing waves, the William Bell, Jr. original was restored by Sanford Ferris Golf Design in 2017. The adjacent Mauka Course (below) was an original John Sanford design with holes benched into steep slopes, preserving the famous Keauhou Holua Slide and providing spectacular views of the Pacific Ocean.

Great Sand Dunes
Alamosa, Colorado

Designed in 1989, the minimalist design approach utilized the natural surrounding and preserved native vegetation. It was an early project John did with Mr. Takahashi that saw both men spending a lot of time on-site to make sure the routing took advantage of site features and minimal shaping enhanced the terrain to create a playable yet strategic course. The course was sold to the Nature Conservancy and closed in 2004.

Relics from the former ranch could be found at Great Sand Dunes along with views of the Rocky Mountains

Mauna Kea creates the backdrop for the 16th hole at Waimea Country Club and is home to the world's largest observatory

Waimea Country Club

Kamuela, Hawaii

Located on Hawaii's Big Island was a unique upland 18-hole public golf course design by John Sanford in the early 1990s. The course was shaped by John's stepbrother Mark Bennett and was once featured in a Golf Channel segment.

"In the early 1990s, one of Mr. Takahashi's adventures was creating Waimea Country Club. He was enamored with the Big Island of Hawaii and had already purchased Kona Country Club and the adjacent hotel. He then purchased about 200 acres in the center of the island, in the town of Kamuela. This was part of the old Parker Ranch and reminded me of a cattle ranch in the western United States. It was up in the mountains at about 3,000 feet above sea level, so it stayed cool and rained a lot. The topography was perfect for a golf course, and the native grass was long and looked like fescue.

"My brother had graduated from University of Hawaii and was working for Mr. T, so naturally he became the 'shaper.' We decided the site called for a Scottish links course complete with kikuyu grass fairways and bentgrass greens. We built that course with Mr. Takahashi's guys from Japan and some local laborers. It was a solid piece of work."
—John Sanford

Garden Valley Golf Club
Lindale, Texas

Designed by John Sanford in 1992, the golf course has been consistently rated as one of the top courses in East Texas.

"Mr. Takahashi was buying or building courses within one hour of major metropolitan areas and selling a corporate membership package to Japanese corporations. Garden Valley was a beautiful piece of golf property with excellent rolling topography, towering East Texas pines and natural lakes. This was a dream come true for a young golf course architect.

"I soon discovered that with dreams come nightmares; the weather around Dallas was brutal. Steaming hot summers, cold, cold winters and rainy springs and falls. The soils appeared to be nice and sandy but we soon found out there was lots of clay under the sand. Every time we rough shaped a hole and plated it with sand, a 'gully washer' would come through and take all the sand to the bottom of the hill. We must have reshaped that course four times.

"On one particular trip to Tyler, I decided to take American Eagle from Dallas instead of driving. I was never fond of prop planes, so I was nervous to begin with. As we left the ground at DFW, the weather was bad and I heard a loud bang in the back of the plane. I immediately thought the worst. The plane dipped and bobbed to a point that made me pray. Oddly the pilot did not try to turn around, and we landed in Tyler after about 25 minutes in the air.

When exiting the aircraft I noticed the cargo door had come off, and the ground guys were in a huddle trying to figure out what the hell had happened. Evidently half of the luggage was somewhere between Dallas and Tyler. The good news is I had carried on my backpack so no luggage lost." —John Sanford

Above: Garden Valley's 11th hole plays along Butler Lake
Below: The par 3, 12th hole

Mt. Takachiho overlooking Regent Miazaki Country Club's 18th hole

Regent Miyazaki Country Club
Miyazaki, Japan

Regent Miyazaki was the second project John built with Mr. Takahashi and the first co-design with golf legend Lee Trevino. The 18-hole golf course was carved out of the rugged terrain of southern Japan. Approximately 2 million cubic yards of earthwork was required to "bench" holes into the steep slopes of the mountains.

3

Imhotep's Footsteps

Maritim Jolie Golf Resort
Sharm El Sheikh, Egypt

This resort golf course was John's first design in Egypt. Completed in 1997, the facility boasts a championship golf course and practice facility. The property was also a resort home to President Mubarak. The Maritim Jolie Golf Resort was developed out of a necessity to stop sending sewer water into Naama Bay, a well-known diving spot.

The golf course was not only the centerpiece for a new resort, but also created a "bio filter" to keep the Naama Bay clean.

"Egypt's Best Golf Resort 2020" —**World Golf Awards**

Little Venice Golf Resort

Ain Sokhna, Egypt

Drive due east from Cairo to the Red Sea and you'll run into the Little Venice Golf Course, featuring nine championship holes with a full-length practice range. The course combines with Sokhna Golf Club, a neighboring 9-hole facility, to play the annual Alps Tour event.

Taba Heights Golf Resort
Taba, Egypt

Taba Heights Golf Resort is located on the northern tip of the Gulf of Aqaba. The course extends from the shoreline to the base of the Sinai Mountains and provides stunning views of the Gulf, Israel, Jordan, and Saudi Arabia.

The 18-hole championship course measures 7,100 yards and is well suited to test golfers of all levels, as each hole offers the option of five different tee placements.

"International Development of the Year" —**Golf Inc. (2008)**

Host to European Tour events

The Gulf of Aqaba, with the mountains of Saudi Arabia in the distance, provides a stunning backdrop for the par 4, 7th hole

Palm Hills Golf Resort
Cairo, Egypt

Just outside Cairo, not far from the Pyramids of Giza, Sanford Golf Design worked with Nicklaus Design to create the premiere golf destination in Egypt.

The resort facility features a spectacular 27-hole golf course with plenty of vertical change, strategic water features and exceptional views, unlike any other golf experience.

To help grow the game in Egypt, the facility offers a golf academy, a short-game area and a practice range that can be set up as a 9-hole, par-3 course.

"Everyone assumes that Egypt is all sand, but most of the sites I worked on were solid lime rock. Palm Hills was one of them. We sited the clubhouse on the high point to give patrons a good view of the Pyramids. There was a steep incline up to the clubhouse so we had a lot of cuts and fills to make those holes work. At one point there were 27 rock hammers on-site cracking the lime rock so it could be moved to fill areas. Once the rough 'rock work' was completed, we needed 1.5 meters of clean sand imported to shape the contours and install irrigation. Good news is... you don't need much drainage when it never rains."
—John Sanford

The Great Pyramids of Giza are a part of Palm Hills Golf Resort's clubhouse vista

Sunset over Madinat Makadi Resort's 1st hole with the mountains of Egypt's Eastern Desert in the distance

Madinat Makadi Resort
Makadi Bay, Egypt

Madinat Makadi Golf Resort on Egypt's Red Sea is the longest course in the region (7,500 yards), with six sets of tees and a 9-hole short course. The course features include lagoons, salt water lakes connected by cascades, and several holes that overlook the exotic coastline of the Red Sea. In addition, the facility features a golf academy with three practice holes and a 3-in-1 practice range.

"Best Course in Egypt" —World Golf Award: 2014, 2015, 2016, 2017, 2018, 2019

Host to international championships

Hacienda Bay Golf Resort
El Alamein, Egypt

Turf area was minimized to conserve water, and the remaining portions of the golf course are desertscape. Salt-tolerant Platinum Paspalum was planted because the water source is a combination of treated effluent and wells, with the local government supplying water as a backup.

The course first entered construction in January 2008, but the development was put on hold after the Arab Spring in 2010. Before construction resumed in 2014, seven holes (one through five, seventeen and eighteen) were redesigned to provide additional land for villas due to the tourism demographic shift post Arab Spring.

"Hacienda Bay is a beautiful location right on the Mediterranean Sea. The beaches and water are some of the most beautiful I've ever seen. This site was also the location of the famous, decisive WWII battle between the Desert Fox and General Montgomery that stopped Rommel on his way to the Suez Canal. It was not out of the ordinary to find unexploded ordnances during earthwork and rough shaping. One day a few laborers found an explosive device and were carrying it around like a football. It was such a common occurrence they thought nothing of it. I found out later that it was a dud... thank God!" —John Sanford

Located on Egypt's North Coast Hacienda Bay is the former site of the Second Battle of El Alamein during WWII

Home Field Advantage

Banyan Golf Club
West Palm Beach, Florida

Working with the club and utilizing historic images and aerial, Sanford Golf Design restored this Joe Lee classic layout in 2012. The restoration received much praise from the members and local golf community.

Hobe Sound Golf Club

Hobe Sound, Florida

Originally designed by Joe Lee in the late 1980s, this South Florida classic was restored by Sanford Golf Design in the early 2000s. Unlike many residential golf communities, homes do not encroach and native habitat was preserved.

The golf course winds its way through a sand ridge populated with native slash pines and palmettos. Lakes were designed to generate fill, complement the natural environment, and enhance strategy.

Hunters Run Country Club
Boynton Beach, Florida

After an extensive planning and design process that included half a dozen workshops with the board of directors, green committee and general membership, club approvals were obtained for the renovation of their North golf course.

Rebuilt during the summer of 2018, the renovated golf course provides improved playability, aesthetics, strategy, drainage and irrigation. The gentle rolling terrain and established trees that line the fairways provide the ideal backdrop for golf in South Florida.

The volcano green complex at Hunter's Run Country Club's par 3, 16th hole

Juliette Falls Golf Club
Dunnellon, Florida

The philosophy we embraced as we staked out the best holes on the 546-acre site was "be gentle on the land." A master plan was created emphasizing the best locations for golf holes and their features while staying true to the site's natural movement.

Cascading waterfalls, smooth fairways and greens make for an exhilarating experience.

"Juliette Falls was a blast. It was the first time my client and I were about the same age. Ron Clapper, aka 'Big Dog,' and I had a great time designing and building the golf course. Gary Kessener, whom I'd worked with at Granite Links, supervised construction. We had a great piece of property and an owner who gave us a 'free hand' to create a great golf experience. To this day I en-

joy returning to Juliette Falls; it's a fun and relaxing place to play golf and hang out." —John Sanford

"Top 10 Best New" —Golf Magazine & Golf Digest

"When you start with a great piece of land and a world-class course architect, you get exceptional results!"
—Ron Clapper, Owner

The par 3, 16th hole at Juliette Falls Golf Club has its risk-reward angle setup by a native area that fronts the green

Naples Beach Hotel was a family owned resort for 75 years located on Florida's Gulf Coast

Naples Beach Hotel & Golf
Naples, Florida

At the Naples Beach Hotel, Sanford Golf Design worked with Jack Nicklaus to renovate the course where Jack first broke 40 for 9 holes as a 10-year-old.

Working with a small 100-acre site, the team was able to stretch the course to over 6,900 yards and created a tee system for players of all levels. A new 300-yard range was also added.

"We started the planning process when the owners, Henry and Mike Watkins, asked if there was a 'signature designer' that I could work with. I immediately said I had worked with Mr. Nicklaus, and there's no better name in the business. The Watkins brothers loved the idea of bringing Jack into the redesign but thought he would be very expensive. The next week I was in the Nicklaus office and ran into Jack. He asked what I was working on, and when I told him the Naples Beach Hotel, his eyes lit up and he said, 'John, that was the first course I broke 40 on when I was 10 years old.' Needless to say, the deal was made and we were on-site with Jack the next week. Nothing like West Palm Beach to Naples on Air Bear in 20 minutes." —John Sanford

"Working with the Sanford team was an excellent experience. The attention to detail and dedication was extremely impressive." —Jason Parsons, GM

Banyan Cay Resort & Golf
West Palm Beach, Florida

This is the site of the former President Country Club, where John Sanford honed his game as a youth.

A collaboration with Jack Nicklaus, the renovated course showcases 25 feet of elevation change, striking landforms, various water features, gentle rolling fairways, five sets of tees and strategic bunkering.

"It was surreal to go back to the courses I grew up on and reimagine the entire project. The 36-hole President Country Club had failed during the Great Recession, and with lots of debt due to clubhouse expansions, the club went back to the bank. My good friend Greg Fagan and his partners bought the property, and during the recession they managed to re-zone one of the two courses for residential and resort development. They then sold the property to the Gatto family for development and redesign of the championship golf course. Mr. Nicklaus was hired as the signature designer, and along with his senior designer, Chris Cochran, we redesigned the South course.

"It was a fairly complex undertaking; since all of the former North golf course was being converted to residential, the soil had to be cleaned up. It involved scraping about two feet of material off of one course and dumping it on the other course being rebuilt. Naturally there was more volume than expected, so we raised the range quite a bit, which actually made it better. I spent lots of time on-site and many memories of working and playing there came flooding back." —John Sanford*

"An exceptional testament to the work Sanford can accomplish. A landmark course created by Jack Nicklaus and John Sanford, with Sanford Golf Design's flawless management of the project." —Domenic Gatto, Owner

Banyan Cay's par 5, 7th hole with its penninsula green provides an exciting risk-reward challenge

Spring Run Golf Club
Bonita Springs, Florida

Working with the club to develop a comprehensive master plan, Sanford Golf Design led the charge to gain membership approval with member workshops and presentations. Overseeing construction every step of the way, our renovation offered improved strategy, aesthetics, infrastructure, sustainability and financial health for the club.

"After the renovation we saw improvement to our bottom line, but increased member satisfaction is greater than the revenue." — Mike Zigler, GM

Spring Run's par 3, 4th hole plays 240 yards from the back tee

Mission Valley Country Club
Nokomis, Florida

Sanford Golf Design developed a long-range plan for course improvements and worked with the club to implement the changes over a five-year period. Creating a road map for course improvements was critical to ensure the project was implemented correctly, stakeholders were informed, phasing could be determined and the project was properly funded.

Pointe West Country Club
Vero Beach, Florida

Rising from an old citrus grove, the course was developed in 1999. Material generated from new lakes was used to build receptive landing areas, rolling fairways and contoured greens. Striking bunkering creates risk/reward strategic shot opportunities. A unique water feature just short of the 18th green makes for a visually exciting and strategic finishing hole.

In 2020 John was invited back to make improvements to the course features that had deteriorated during its 20-year existence, the first time John would renovate his own course.

Wilderness Country Club
Naples, Florida

Designed by Art Hills in the 1970s, Wilderness Country Club is fittingly named. As you enter the gated community, you will be struck by the majestic trees and native landscape that dominate the property.

Restorations don't always fit financial and market analysis, but when a club decides to be the custodians of classic design, our appreciation for golf course design history sets us apart. We owe it to the game to preserve and restore the best designs of the architects who preceded us.

Wilderness Country Club's signature 15th hole features a bunker within the green

The par 3, 8th hole at Eastpointe Country Club's East Course

Eastpointe Country Club
Palm Beach Gardens, Florida

Eastpointe Country Club was originally designed by George Fazio in 1974. Sanford Golf Design's 2007 restoration of this well-loved course is reminiscent of "Old Florida" and provides a stunning backdrop for some exceptional golf. It remains a local favorite and one we are proud to have in our hometown.

> *"Sanford Golf Design has done a very good job preserving the integrity of the golf course, addressing member concerns, and balancing the post-improvement maintenance requirements, all while working closely with the golf course superintendent."* —John Spiwak, Director of Golf Course Grounds

Miami Shores Country Club
Miami Shores, Florida

The 1939 Red Lawrence course is listed on the Florida Historic Golf Trail. Historic aerial and pictures were used to create detailed plans for the greens and bunkers. Tees were redesigned to accommodate today's players.

Wycliffe Golf & Country Club
Wellington, Florida

The East and West Golf Courses were redesigned to create a contrasting native aesthetic on the West Course versus the more ornate East Course. The comprehensive renovation of the West Course eliminated a par-3 starting hole, multiple road crossings, poor cart routing and poorly drained fairways.

Pembroke Lakes Golf Club

Pembroke Pines, Florida

Seeing the immense value in redesigning, dedicated city leaders selected Sanford and Champions Tour player Bruce Fleisher to improve their decades-old course. The renovation has made it a favorite among locals and visitors alike. It serves as a prime example of how upgrading a public course can pay dividends to the municipality.

"John Sanford and his entire team did a fantastic job on the total redo of the Pembroke Lakes Golf Course. He was fully engaged from beginning to the total completion of the project. His on-site, hands-on involvement ensured that the course was perfect in every measured category. John is professional, courteous, cooperative, and showed great expertise. The rounds and revenues grew over 40 percent during the first year after the renovation and have continued to be successful based on the quality product that we now offer. I would highly recommend John Sanford, as our company would not consider anyone else for future projects. He's that good."
—Johnny Lopanzina, President, Professional Course Management

Pembroke Lakes Golf Club's 6th green in the forground and 10th green in the distance

Atlantis Golf Club
Atlantis, Florida

Atlantis Golf Club was originally designed by Bill Mitchell, John's childhood neighbor who introduced him to golf course design. In the early 2000s, John got to restore Bill's North and South courses, and make improvements to the poorly drained East course, allowing the club to remain relevant for years afterward.

Breakers West Country Club
West Palm Beach, Florida

Working with PGA Tour player Ken Green, John Sanford rerouted several holes, and made improvements to the golf course. The redesign of the golf course also afforded the owner with additional real estate opportunities and helped establish Breakers West Country Club as a premier South Florida private golf community.

Vero Beach Country Club
Vero Beach, Florida

Sanford Ferris Golf Design renovated all 18 holes of this 1924 Herbert Strong original. As the Vero Beach Country Club's architect since the 1990s, we have continued to work with the club on improvements to their Audubon-certified golf course.

Vero Beach Country Club's 11th hole wraps around native areas and lake to create a stunning visual composition

Madison Green Country Club
Royal Palm Beach, Florida

The 18-hole championship golf course incorporates large lakes, including an eight-acre aqua range. The course is best known for its greens and strategic layout with exciting challenges for golfers at every turn. The spectacular design, coupled with extraordinary conditions, sets this golfing experience apart from others.

"Best New Public Golf Course" —Florida Golf Magazine

"Top 20 Best New Courses in America" —Golf Magazine

"4¾ out of 5 Stars" —Golf Digest & Golf Magazine

The finishing hole at Madison Green offers exciting risk-reward oppotunities with its bunker, lakes, and native area

———————————— 5 ————————————

Around-the-Horn

Apple Mountain
Freeland, Michigan

Incorporating a ski hill built on a man-made landform in the otherwise flat central region of Michigan, with an apple orchard and a routing sensitive to existing wetlands and vegetation, a championship golf course was expertly shaped into the land. The course is highlighted by nine ponds and large bunkers that cover almost nine acres.

Some of the most strategic bunkering is found on hole 13, where a huge bunker sets up the tee shot angle, requiring a riskier longer shot for the best approach to the green on the second shot.

"Apple Mountain was a tourist attraction of sorts. The former owner had pushed up a large mountain of dirt and made a ski hill that was popular amongst snowboarders back then. When planning the project, we were trying to maximize residential lots without hindering the golf course, so we sited the practice range to hit up the slope on the ski hill, which allowed us to get some additional lots and have plenty of space for the course. We used the back side of the ski hill for a dramatic downhill par 3. It was a nice run in Michigan in the 1990s, with The Quest in Houghton Lake, The Sawmill and Apple Mountain. Lots of great people that were a pleasure to work with and liked to have a good time. I miss that place." —John Sanford

Apple Mountain's par 3, 5th hole with its iconic apple shaped green complex

The serpentine bunker runs from tee to green at the Quest Golf Club's par 4, 9th hole

The Quest Golf Club

Houghton Lake, Michigan

This 1994 co-design with PGA Tour player Ken Green (pictured on-site with John) features five sets of tees and plays anywhere from 6,800 yards to 4,900 yards to accommodate all levels of play.

"It was early in my career and Ken was a good friend, so we had lots of fun designing and building the course. Kenny had a bunch of good ideas and it was my job to incorporate them into the design. Wadsworth Construction was the contractor and they had some talented guys on the job. In the summer months we would work until nine o'clock and then go out for din-

ner and drinks. Loved those summers in Michigan!" —John Sanford

"Top Courses You Can Play" **—Golf Digest**

The Sawmill
Saginaw, Michigan

The Sawmill is a premier golf course located in Saginaw Township, surrounded by exquisite homes, where a unique golf experience is the rule, not the exception.

The golf course incorporates natural wetlands, pine groves and strategic bunkering. Designed in 1997 by John Sanford, it also features a practice facility for all aspects of the game.

The Brookside Club

Bourne, Massachusetts

Owned by old family friends, the picturesque course on Cape Cod was renovated by John Sanford in 1996. The golf course stands out as a public course that offers significant elevation change, wonderful views of Buzzards Bay and a fun yet challenging course that feels more like a private club.

The back nine at Caguas Real is routed along the foothills of Puerto Rico's Cordillera Central mountian range

Caguas Real
Caguas, Puerto Rico

Set into the mountainous region in Central Puerto Rico, the back nine holes are benched into steep slopes, while the front nine is routed through the flat areas to the north. The course was designed and built in the early 2000s.

"My first official 'design/build' job was working with Frontier Construction on a site in Caguas, Puerto Rico, about an hour south of San Juan. The course was in the middle of a large development that included hotels, restaurants, villas, etc.

"The developer, Jose Ventura, was a flamboyant and somewhat famous character in Puerto Rico. During construction he was indicted, found guilty of racketeering, and received a one-year jail sentence. I received a call from Nick Sigliano at Frontier saying don't worry; we will finish the job and Jose will pay us when he gets out. I was blown away that Nick would take this chance, risking millions. My part was just a small percentage, but I was impressed by Nick's confidence. We finished the job and were paid shortly after Mr. Ventura's release. I have ultimate respect for Nick and his guys for finishing the project." —John Sanford

Duxbury Yacht Club
Duxbury, Massachusetts

The Duxbury Yacht Club, located in the South Shore region near Boston, Massachusetts, was founded in 1875 and is one of the oldest yacht clubs in America. The club's golf course opened in 1901 as a 6-hole layout. Wayne Stiles expanded the course to nine holes in the 1920s, and in 1969 another nine holes were added by Geoffrey Cornish.

"My family goes back decades at Duxbury Yacht Club; we lived there in the early 60s during the off-season, and my dad would hit colored golf balls in the snow before they were popular. In 2008 we were hired to create a long-range master plan for DYC, and each year the club would pick away at whatever limited work they could fit into the budget. Little projects like tree removal, green enlargement and cart path repair were getting done in the off-season, but no real significant and noticeable improvements were made. Through the persistence of Head Pro Randy Grills and Commodore David Hallowell, a major renovation plan was finally approved in 2019.

"The course was an interesting design mix of Wayne Stiles' front nine and Geoffrey Cornish's back nine. The front was generally more interesting due to the topography and landscape; the back nine was down in the flatter flood plain with fewer trees. This was a project that I thought would never happen, but we ended up transforming the two different nines into one cohesive golf course. All the bunkers were rebuilt, and many former bunkers that had disappeared over the years were brought back into play. Aesthetics were enhanced by removing overgrown trees and introducing new fescue areas in the deep rough. It was a pleasure to work on a course with the old family ties and finally complete the job after so many years. It's always nice to go back to our roots." — John Sanford

Duxbury Yacht Club 18th hole sits along Massachusetts' South Shore, originally holes designed by Wayne Stiles in the 1920's

Reclamation

Landfills are not known for their beauty, but for John, who uses them as canvas for artistic creation, beauty is in the eye of the beholder. His two once-in-a-life-time landfill projects, Granite Links and Trump Golf Links at Ferry Point, helped redefine reclamation golf course design.

Granite Links (Boston, Massachusetts)

Entangled with the "American Dream" that blossomed out of the post–World War II era was a love affair with the automobile, suburban living and the inter-states that connected it to urban centers. Many of America's great cities were dis-sected by multi-lane highways, and by the late 1980s, cities were seeking rem-edies.

Boston, which found itself cut off from its own waterfront by I-93, determined the best solution was to bury the highway underground with a se-ries of connected tunnels. This monumental con-cept presented many engineering challenges, but the biggest was the excavation of a large volume of material; hence the project's nickname, the "Big Dig." Planners of the 1990s' largest U.S. civil works project proposed shipping the material to Springfield or building a small island in the harbor. Enter Charles "Chick" Geilich, with his wild idea that would save taxpayers hundreds of millions of dollars by using the fill to build a golf course.

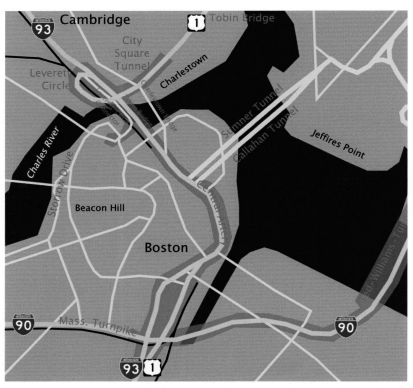

Construction sites of the Big Dig

John recalls,

"In the early 1990s I was introduced to Chick, who was from Boston and had a place in Jupiter, Florida, for the winter. He was looking for a golf course architect to help him with a wild idea. Chick had been in the disposal business and thought the exca-vated material could be taken to the Quincy landfill just six miles away. He met with a few architects, but evidently I was the only one willing to indulge in such a wild plan."

Like others of its era, the Quincy and Milton land-fill's future uses were never contemplated, as landfills are typically perceived as just an eyesore. In the 1980s municipalities began developing passive parks to better utilize closed landfills, but that was confined to the flat areas on top. At Granite Links they wanted to do something different, so along with a picnic area, trails and a clubhouse restaurant that offered breathtaking views of the Boston skyline, they incorporated more active uses such as baseball and soccer fields.

By taking all of the Big Dig material we were able to recontour the entire site, including the steep slopes. The result was something resembling a wedding cake, with golf holes benched into the side of the landfill domes.

The initial plans involved an 18-hole golf complex

The site's old quarry mines, one of the country's largest producers of granite and favorite local swimming hole once featured on the cover of *Life* magazine

on the Quincy landfill, but during design development the Town of Milton offered their adjacent landfill, and the project grew to 36 holes. Despite the symbiotic relations with state and federal agencies that saved the tunnel project millions, they still required 80-plus permits. The site's existing wetlands, old quarries, Blue Hills Reservation viewshed, settling and methane venting also proved challenging, but once the Massachusetts Historical Society got involved, everything slowed

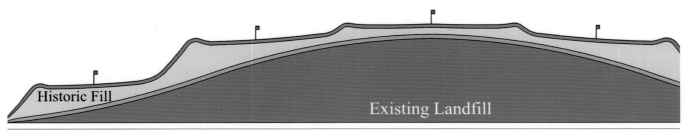

Historic Fill

Existing Landfill

Diagram of the terraces John was able to build on the side of the landfill with the large volume of fill

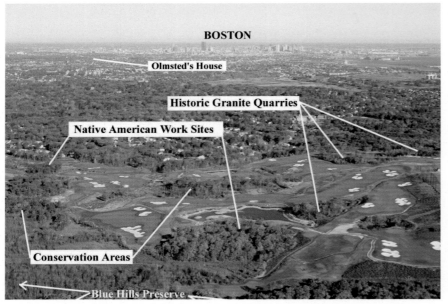

Site constraints required the utmost sensitivity when designing the golf course

and irrigation system) had to be installed without disturbing the landfill's "seal."

To garner the best views, a clubhouse was built on top of the landfill. Huge pilings that penetrate the trash layer and sit on the bedrock far below the surface were required. A methane venting and monitoring system was designed throughout the structure. To thousands who use it as their community gathering place with spectacular views of the ninth green and the Boston skyline, it offers more than just the typical utilitarian purposes.

down. The course had to be redesigned and reduced to 27 holes to preserve the "prehistoric Native American workshops" after arrowheads were discovered.

Once the plans and permits were in place, the logistics of moving the 800–1,000 trucks a day for five years from downtown Boston to the Quincy

Site-specific details and construction methods were developed so the existing landfill capping was not compromised, methane venting systems were removed from activity areas, water was not allowed to pool on or below the surface and settling was mitigated.

The landfill was "closed" and capped with specific layers and depths of material. Each of the layers had to feather into the edges of the wetlands, skirt the historic worksites, allow for the collection of gases and prevent grading of golf course features. Infrastructure (drainage

Golf course being shaped on the Milton landfill with the huge mounds of excavated material from the Big Dig being stockpiled and tested on the Quincy landfill

landfill created problems, as trucks could only access the site by driving through town. John remembers Chick and his partners appeasing the upset citizens of Quincy by achieving the unthinkable.

"They proposed a new exit directly off the expressway and straight into the landfill site. Up to then the state average time for design, permitting and construction of an off-ramp was about seven years. Low and behold the partners achieved the same feat in seven months, and for about 10 percent of the typical cost. This caused a lot of commotion at the state capital." — John Sanford

Unlike other golf courses built in this era, it was designed with significantly reduced maintained turf area, lower impact irrigation heads and a drainage system that contained runoff to create something that was both unique and sustainable.

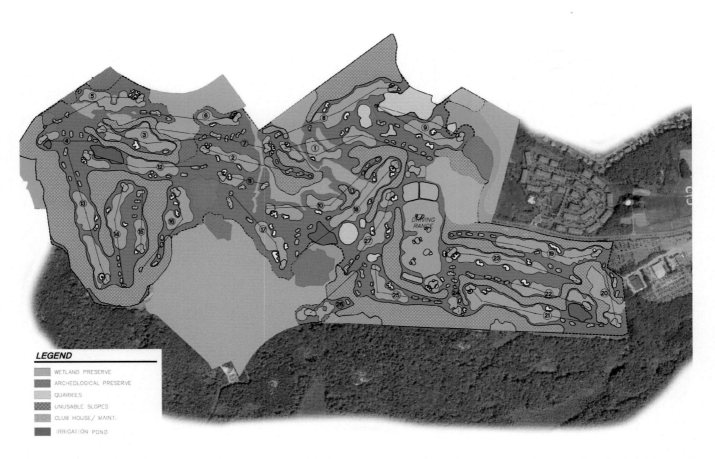

LEGEND
- WETLAND PRESERVE
- ARCHEOLOGICAL PRESERVE
- QUARRIES
- UNUSABLE SLOPES
- CLUB HOUSE/ MAINT.
- IRRIGATION POND

Granite Links Master Plan, showing the course layout and project constraints, including wetlands, archeological preserves and abandoned quarries

The 7th hole at Granite Links, playing over preserved wetlands in the lower portion of the site

John, Gary Kessener (Construction Manager for Granite Links, Trump Golf Links and Juliette Falls), Fred Funk (PGA Tour), and Dave Ferris at the grand opening of Juliette Falls GC near Ocala, FL

This innovative approach has allowed the course to use less fertilizers, pesticides and water.

During construction and the grow-in period of the course, surface drainage and runoff on the site presented other challenges. An extensive stormwater management program was implemented to protect wetlands and other ecological features within the complex and nearby residential areas. The design of the course allowed about 65 percent of the runoff from irrigation and storms to be recovered for reuse on the course.

The par-3 15th hole, with the Blue Hills Reservation as backdrop

The renowned golf facility has gone on to host professional golf tournaments and is a favorite of local residents and visitors alike, but from its inception the project has always been more than just a golf course. It grew out of a public call to improve our inner cities and has proven to be a long-term environmental, economic and social benefit for the entire community.

Sanford Golf Design was able to create a public course that was ranked "Top Courses in New England," "Top 100 Public Courses in America" and "Best New Course in America," received the American Society of Golf Course Architect's Design Excellence Award and the American Society of Landscape Architects–FL Merit Award.

John with Chick Geilich receiving ASGCA's Design Excellence Award

"SGD's attention to detail and patience to solve problems throughout design and construction allowed this spectacular golf experience to come to life." —Chick Geilich, Owner/Partner

The 16th hole at Granite Links with a stunning view to the Boston skyline offers a unique risk/reward tee shot

Trump Golf Links at Ferry Point (Bronx, New York)

If you have ever traveled to the Bronx over New York City's Whitestone Bridge, you have probably noticed a large green open space known as Ferry Point Park. Within that 400-acre park is a 170-acre parcel home to an 18-hole championship links-style golf course co-designed by Jack Nicklaus, John Sanford and Jim Lipe.

The entire Ferry Point Park is approximately half the size of Central Park and was originally developed as part of the Throgmorton Grant of 1642. The park gained notoriety, and its name, for the ferries that traveled between the Bronx and Queens from 1910 to 1939. In the 1930s, parcels throughout New

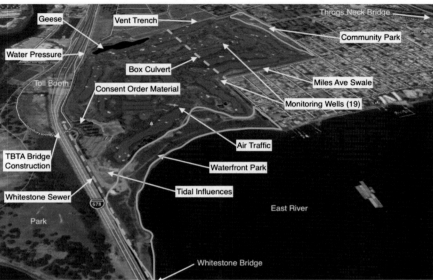

Diagram depicting the various site constraints at Ferry Point

York City were acquired as part of Robert Moses' vision for interconnecting the area's islands and mainland. The Whitestone Bridge, which dissects Ferry Point Park, was a key component of that vision. In 1948, the park was expanded by condemnation and then converted into a landfill. The Sanitation Department operated the site until 1970. The ground lay fallow into the late 1990s, when the city's Parks Department attempted to convert the landfill to a golf course.

In early 2008, when golf course projects were coming to a screeching halt, I came across a request for proposal (RFP) from New York City

1930's Ferry Point Park with the Whitestone Bridge was under construction

Conceptual rendering for the 17th hole

that seemed like a perfect fit. Mayor Bloomberg was interested in converting an old landfill next to the East River and Whitestone Bridge in the Bronx into a championship golf course that would challenge the likes of Bethpage Black.

As John recalls,

> *"We had recently completed Granite Links, so we decided to go after the project, utilizing our unique landfill experience."*

Arriving to the site a few hours early for the city's pre-bid meeting, I was able to gain a better understanding of the site and had a chance encounter with the project manager who was overseeing the importation of fill material. Upon discovering this was an active construction site, I asked the next

logical question: "How do you know where to put the fill material without any plans?" That's when he pulled out a set of old Nicklaus Design plans. I called John and asked him what he thought about adding Mr. Nicklaus to our team. John had a long-standing friendship with the Nicklaus family and was able to work out a collaboration deal with them. I'm not sure there are many others Jack would have teamed up with for such a project, a testament to the respect Jack and other architects have for John.

According to John,

> *"We were fortunate to be shortlisted with two or three other firms; I believe there were over 30 proposals submitted, so we felt very lucky. As we prepared for the presentation,*

we realized that Mr. Nicklaus had started a design on the site years before but it never got off the ground. I also realized that we needed some cache to come out on top. I contacted Nicklaus Design and they joined the team. Little did we know we were about to enter the twilight zone for the next five years."

As project managers, making it through the nine-month process to complete the three phases of the RFP process and contract negotiations with the city was very challenging and proved to be the warm-up act for the next five years. The project

bring this amazing project to fruition.

"Our contract with New York City was as tall as the Whitestone Bridge," John said. *"Honestly, I had no idea what we were in for, but somehow Dave and I would make it work. We had an over-regulated site, a dysfunctional client, a contractor with zero golf course experience, a high-profile project, and a huge learning curve to understand the 'nuances' of working in New York City. Let's just say I could write a separate book about this one."*

The pre-bid meeting, which attracted more than 50 participants, of which 30 golf course architects submitted for the project

had a cast of characters that looked like something out of a Hollywood set: the billionaire mayor, a real estate developer who would go on to be President of the United States, the greatest golfer of all time, a legal team accustomed to manipulating contract language to meet whatever need arose, and plenty of other quirky characters. Through it all, it was an honor to work with our 12 subconsultants and

THE CONCEPT—From a land use perspective, a landfill golf course makes sense because few other large tracts are available in the midst of our population centers. Municipalities reap added benefits, as a golf course dresses up an eyesore and provides a valued amenity to residents. Housing and most types of commercial uses are not suitable for former landfills. Golf courses are often cheaper to build and maintain, from an environmental perspective, than open-space parks. In addition, they provide jobs for the community, a recreation hub for social activities and revenue for the municipality.

Sanford Golf Design worked with Jack Nicklaus to design a links-style golf course with tall, blowing native grasses and dunes with teeing grounds that rise as high as 50 feet and provide splendid views of the East River and the Manhattan skyline. Mayor Bloomberg specifically intended the par-71 course, at 7,200 yards from the back tees, to be worthy of PGA Tour events and major championships.

When asked about the golf course during its construction, Jack Nicklaus said,

> *"A course like this sends a message that the City of New York has made a huge effort to build something very special. The course absolutely could handle majors, but we are more concerned with what everyday public players think."*

THE NUTS AND BOLTS—As with any golf course designed atop a landfill, there are special challenges to be addressed, such as infrastructure, landfill closure requirements, permit approvals, methane monitoring, differential settlement, erosion control during construction, post grow-in runoff, wetlands, and water quality. Add changing environmental regulations during the design and con-

struction phases and the process becomes more complex. In addition, the Ferry Point excavation was kept to a minimum to reduce the impacts of the Department of Environmental Conservation (DEC) requirements that unearthed municipal

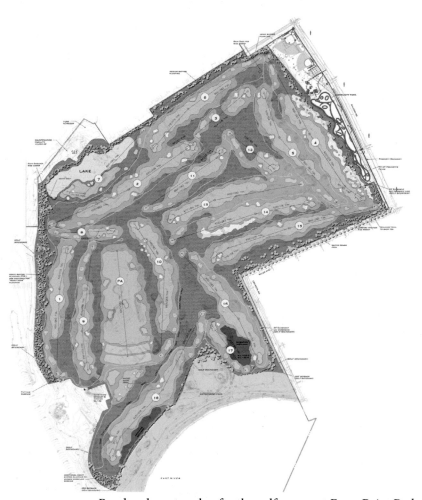

Rendered master plan for the golf course at Ferry Point Park

solid waste be removed from the site. This resulted in more than 2.4 million cubic yards of fill and cover material to be imported.

> *"The city had been bringing fill material to this site for 14 years,"* John said. *"So we had plenty of material to create landforms*

The once derelict landfill within NYC's Ferry Point Park, transformed into an 18-hole Irish links–style golf course

emulating an Irish links course. I think that separates this golf course from others. Shaping the landforms to the strategy that Jack supplied us created risk/reward possibilities to make it special."

An integral part of building this golf course was the "closing" of the landfill and meeting all DEC regulations. Methane gas was vented to reduce potential release of harmful gases into the atmosphere and avoid internal combustion. Vents were placed inconspicuously throughout the site in the outer rough's links-style mounding. In addition, 20 monitoring wells were installed to facilitate DEC's requirement for continual monitoring of methane and groundwater.

Deep dynamic compaction rig and the craters it creates in the background

The differential settling that can occur from decomposing trash below was mitigated in key feature areas of the golf course with deep dynamic compaction. Additionally, all tees and greens are supported by massive "substructures" that prevent differential settling. These substructures extend 10 feet beyond the tees and greens and are comprised of 12-inch and 18-inch coarse aggregate layers placed between "type 3" geogrid and covered with a composite liner system.

More than 2 million cubic yards of bulk fill was imported to Ferry Point Park to sculpt the golf course, but this material was not acceptable as "final cover" material. To meet DEC regulations and provide a

Moving stockpiled material during the early stages of construction

quality growing medium for the links-style course, approximately 400,000 cubic yards of sandy cover material had to be spread across the entire golf course at a minimum 12-inch depth. DEC also required a "demarcation layer" placed between the base grade and cover material. For this project, the approved demarcation material was common orange "snow fence," which was installed in all areas where final grade was within four feet of municipal solid waste.

A red Cornell Alumni hat helps the author stand out. From left to right: Tony McCary (NYC Parks), Dave Ferris, Jim Lipe (Nicklaus Design), Jack Nicklaus, Ron Lieberman (executive vice president at the Trump Organization) and Greg Eisner (superintendent)

To accommodate DEC's restriction on water seeping into the trash, more than 80,000 lineal feet of subsurface drainage was installed. This intricate system delivers subsurface drainage water to the city's master drainage system via the 300 catch basins on the golf course.

All ponds and drainage detention areas were lined with an impervious liner to prevent water from percolating into the trash layer below. Active and passive venting systems were designed to alleviate the buildup of methane gases under the liners. Micro pools and channels were incorporated into the design of the ponds to improve sediment retention.

Anything can happen in New York City. As John recalls,

Jack Nicklaus and John Sanford, on-site at Trump Golf Links at Ferry Point, one of several projects John had the privilege to collaborate on with Jack

"During one site visit, Dave and I were there with Jim [Lipe] and Jack [Nicklaus]. We were discussing the rough shape of the 16th green; the East

River was in the background, so we wanted to keep the view to the river and keep the green elevated for strategic purposes. There was productive conversation between Jack, Jim and me while Dave videotaped the interaction—normal collaborative conversation that led to a sound solution. We thought it made for a good social media post, so Dave put it on YouTube for all to view. Next thing you know we are being threatened with lawsuits by the contractor and the City of New York for causing delays to the project. This issue was a nightmare for several months and took many man-

A screen capture from the infamous YouTube video

hours to resolve, just one of hundreds of challenging issues on the project."

There was so much infrastructure required due to the landfill's constrains and regulatory requirements that it took a couple of years before the site started to look like a golf course.

The par-4 9th hole, with the Whitestone Bridge as backdrop

Bird's-eye view at sunrise with the Whitestone Bridge, East River and Manhattan skyline in the distance

According to John,

"There was a tremendous amount of infrastructure required to build the course, so it took more time than the typical construction period. In 2011 we were actually grading the course and it was starting to take shape, in a good way."

John with Jack Nicklaus, Mayor Bloomberg and Donald Trump at the opening

During construction the city solicited bids for a concessionaire to maintain the golf course, run golf operations and build a clubhouse. The finalists were the PGA Tour and the Trump Organization.

At the time they were selected, golf course construction was approximately 60 percent complete.

As John recalls,

"Honestly, I was in favor of the PGA Tour at the time, but Trump was selected because of their prior successes in New York City."

"Once they were onboard, the project started to move along faster. We could see a clear path to the finish line. Mr. Trump was already pushing for a U.S. Open, and I received an invitation to attend a meeting at Trump Tower with, you guessed it, The Donald, Mr. Nicklaus, Mike Davis, Tom O'Toole and assorted other dignitaries from the city and USGA." —John Sanford

The par-5 15th hole, offering stunning views of the Manhattan skyline

I recall the preparation work involved for that meeting. There was a bound presentation with pictures of the holes that were completed. I received comments from Mr. Trump and worked with his staff to finalize the material. While I was not in attendance, John described the event:

"We were all waiting in 'the boardroom' when Donald walked in with Ivanka; she was eight months pregnant. I was at the far end of the room and watched Donald as he greeted each guest by name, shaking hands and asking how they were doing. I thought, 'This will be interesting; he doesn't know me from Adam.' When he finally reached me, he shook my hand and said 'John... it's great to meet you; you're doing a great job out there and we truly appreciate it!' In 30 seconds, I went from a critic to a fan, just like that."

John added,

"Mr. Trump and his people were great to work with and helped immensely. Unfortunately, when Donald entered the presidential race in 2015, negotiations for a major championship with the USGA and PGA ended for Ferry Point. In the end the course came out very well and we are proud to be part of Mayor Bloomberg's vision."

The project was a marathon of high hurdles, with John carrying the baton. It was so demanding that there was little room for us to take on other projects. Our typical day involved hours of emails,

reviewing reports, budgets, schedules, requests, drawings, addressing project issues and a string of conference calls, all riddled with little sense of accomplishment and a lot of frustration. John was tasked with doing the impossible, but his unique experience at Granite Links and dealing with difficult conditions encountered on international projects, in the author's humble opinion, made him the best golf course architect for the job at Trump Golf Links at Ferry Point.

The golf course opened for public play in 2015 and has received many accolades, including "Top Municipal Golf Courses in America" and "Best New Courses in America." It also received the American Society of Golf Course Architect's Design Excellence Award, Solid Waste Association of North America's Excellence Award for Landfill Redevelopment and the American Society of Landscape Architects–FL Award of Excellence and their coveted Environmental Sustainability Award.

Always nice to get a thank-you note from the president

Epilogue

"When I was very young, my father told me to 'find something you love and make it your life's work.' Luckily I listened to him once in a while.

"Fortunately, one of our neighbors, Bill Mitchell, was a golf course architect, and his son was a friend of mine. I was 12 and had recently started playing golf, and I had no idea there was actually a profession called golf course architecture. One day while at their house for lunch, I noticed a set of plans on the dining room table. I was intrigued and started looking at them. It became obvious the drawings were of golf holes, and I thought, 'What a cool way to make a living.' From that moment forward that's what I wanted to do. Sure I had dreams of playing professionally but always knew that if I worked hard enough I could make a living designing and building courses.

"Designing golf courses has been a 'labor of love,' and although there are some tough days, like in any business, I am blessed to make a living in golf course architecture. The profession has afforded me the opportunity to travel the world, experience various cultures and meet some incredible people along the way. Fortunately, most of the folks in this field are great people with a common goal to produce the best possible product given the site conditions, budget and long-term sustainability.

"A large part of my professional advancement is due to my membership and participation in the American Society of Golf Course Architects. From the time I decided to make it my life's work, I wanted to don the Ross tartan plaid jacket and surpassed my dreams when I became the president of this incredible organization in 2017. I know of no other professional organization with a finer group of members who compete for precious work yet collaborate and assist one another when called upon. It is truly a special organization.

"Thanks to David Ferris for his incredible dedication to our profession and our business. Dave has made it possible for us to remain relevant and function efficiently over the past 25 years. I look forward to the next 25!

"Finally, a special thanks to my family and the people not mentioned in this book who have helped me along this journey. The best is yet to come." —John Sanford